BETHANY KEY

MANIPULATION TECHNIQUES

The ultimate guide to learning how to recognize dark psychology techniques and use the secrets of emotional intelligence and influence to your advantage

© Copyright 2021 - All rights reserved.

The content contained within this book may not be reproduced, duplicated or transmitted without direct written permission from the author or the publisher. Under no circumstances will any blame or legal responsibility be held against the publisher, or author, for any damages, reparation, or monetary loss due to the information contained within this book. Either directly or indirectly.

Legal Notice: This book is copyright protected. This book is only for personal use. You cannot amend, distribute, sell, use, quote or paraphrase any part, or the content within this book, without the consent of the author or publisher.

Disclaimer Notice: Please note the information contained within this document is for educational and entertainment purposes only. All effort has been executed to present accurate, up to date, and reliable, complete information. No warranties of any kind are declared or implied. Readers acknowledge that the author is not engaging in the rendering of legal, financial, medical or professional advice. The content within this book has been derived from various sources. Please consult a licensed professional before attempting any techniques outlined in this book.

By reading this document, the reader agrees that under no circumstances is the author responsible for any losses, direct or indirect, which are incurred as a result of the use of information contained within this document, including, but not limited to, errors, omissions, or inaccuracies.

TABLE OF CONTENTS

INTRODUCTION 3

CHAPTER 1 THE VICTIM 5

How Manipulators Affect Your Behavior 5
Why you are manipulated 12
How to avoid being manipulated 14
Dealing with a Toxic Person 16
Setting Boundaries to Eliminate Manipulators 17
Effect of Toxic People on Your Life 17
Dealing with Manipulators Who Are A Permanent Part Of Your Life 17

CHAPTER 2 WHAT IS MANIPULATION? WHY MANIPULATION IS WRONG & WHY PEOPLE MANIPULATE 20

What is Manipulation 20
The manipulation ethics – could manipulation be good and bad? 23
Why Are We Vulnerable to Manipulation? 25
Why Do People Use Manipulation? 27
What are people's reasons for manipulating others? 28
Different Types Of Negative Manipulation 30
Examples of Manipulation 31

CHAPTER 3 MANIPULATION TACTICS 33

Best manipulation techniques 33

CHAPTER 4 HOW TO HELP SOMEONE BEING CONTROLLED 45

Combatting Manipulation 50

CHAPTER 5 DEALING WITH CONTROLLING PEOPLE 52

How to Deal with a Manipulative Person 52

CONCLUSION 61

Introduction

Every aspect of human life has two sides-positive and negative, but it depends on the human how he or she utilizes it for their good as well as for others. Consider manipulation as a part of dark psychology, and it is used greatly for the wrongdoings and harmful deeds. On the other hand, it can be utilized positively as well, but it's all in your hand how you want to utilize it. As far as persuasion is concerned, people use it in every field and part of life. For example, a salesman will always try to persuade you to buy his or her recommended product even if you do not want to. Persuasion also has two aspects of being applied. If you try to persuade a person to do something illegal or unethical, that is part of dark psychology but if you persuade someone to get out or leave a certain thing that is not beneficial in any means, let's say suicide, then you are using it for the purpose of good. Everything you do or perceive is totally in the human mind, and you are the controller of it. If you don't want to, then no one can make you do things without your will and consent. Also, it is an essential part of living life to observe your surroundings and the people who are around you. If you do not notice the small things and interpret them wisely, then you are more likely to fall prey for something negative and hazardous. Facial expressions, body language, gestures, and the words and tone used, can predict a lot about people if observed closely. If you fail to recognize such signals that are inclined towards negativity, then you will be unable to keep yourself safe from them. Dark psychology is considered to start from the point where you have no intent or motive to do things except for your self-satisfaction and pleasure, and in return, it is damaging to the other person or even the community. Every living individual has this dark side, but not all of them let that side overcome them. Once you are exposed to that side, there is no coming back. So always watch yourself and your surroundings so that you can keep yourself off of any harm. Persuasion, manipulation, and other forms of influence are ubiquitous. You can pick up on some obvious signs here and there, but there are also hidden secret ways that others control you which you might never be able to fully comprehend.

To those who aren't fully aware of manipulation and what it is all about, it is hard to see that this process takes up three steps. Most of us will just think of manipulation as one thing—there needs to be two things in addition to the act of manipulation, which will make sure that the manipulation is successful. Perhaps you are trying to sell something, maybe yourself or your brand, and you need to figure out how to get people to be more persuaded by you to help you achieve the things that you want in this life. No matter where you are or what you are trying to do, you have all the tools that you will ever need to be persuasive or influential with you already.

Before getting into this book, there are a few things that you need to know to be introduced to this topic to get into the right mindset as you read through this text. First, understand that there are no two manipulators that are alike. There are no two easily persuaded people that are the same either. Though it might seem like this sometimes, especially since you can influence a group all at once, you can't let yourself fall into a thinking pattern where you place everyone in the same category.

Don't blame yourself for not being aware of the ways that you have been manipulated in the past. Regret isn't going to do you any good in this journey, so it's best to leave those feelings of, "I wish I would have known this sooner," behind. All that you can do now is move forward, and we will help you every step of the way!

Chapter 1

The Victim

HOW MANIPULATORS AFFECT YOUR BEHAVIOR

Have you ever had that impression in one of the relationships you have that something was not, quite right? Even with a casual gathering with someone you just met. Something just didn't feel quite right, and you are left feeling far more anxious, irritated, or confused than you were when you began. That could be a sign you have been in a manipulator's presence. The reason manipulators use the tactics they do is because they are often unable to simply ask what they need or be able to express their needs in a healthy, straightforward manner. Thus, they resort to this emotionally abusive tactic to try to manipulate other people around them and compel them to bend to their will.

Manipulation comes in various forms, and it can range from abusive to just being around a bossy personality anywhere. Some deceptive habits are much easier to spot than others, and if you believe you may be a psychological bully's target, these are the tell-tale signs for which you want to keep an eye out for:

YOU SENSE FEAR, DUTY, AND GUILT

Coercive conduct comprises three factors: anxiety, responsibility, and guilt. When someone manipulates you, you're mentally coerced to do something that you usually don't want to do. You could feel afraid to do so, compelled to do so, or guilty of not doing so.

I refer to two different manipulators: "the abuser" and "the victim." An abuser makes you feel afraid and will use violence, threats, and coercion to manipulate you. The victim instills a sense of guilt in their target. Usually, the victim acts hurt, although, the fact is they're the ones who created the problem.

An individual approached by a manipulator who acts as the victim always attempts to support the manipulator to avoid feeling bad. Targets of this type of manipulation frequently feel responsible for assisting the victim to stop their suffering by doing everything they can.

STRINGS ARE CONNECTED

If you don't get a favor just because, then it's not "for fun and free. "If strings are applied, then it is trickery.

One manipulator form is "Mr. Nice man". This person will be supportive and offer other people plenty of favors. It's complicated, but you don't know there is anything bad. But, on the other side, there is a rope connected for any positive deed — an obligation. If you don't fulfill the standards of the manipulator, you'll be forced to feel ungrateful. One of the most common forms of trickery is to exploit the rules and standards of reciprocity.

For example, a salesman could make it appear like you would purchase the product since he or she offered you a discount. A spouse in a partnership can buy you flowers and then ask for something in return. These techniques operate as it violates societal expectations. It's normal to return the favor but we often still feel it necessary to reciprocate and comply even if someone does one insincerely.

Manipulators frequently try out one of two strategies. The first one is the strategy of foot-in-the-door, in which somebody starts with a simple yet rational request — like, do you have a moment? — Which then contributes to a bigger request — like I want 10 dollars for a taxi. That's commonly used in street frauds.

The door-in-the-face method is the opposite — it includes somebody making a large request, having it rejected, and then asking a smaller favor.

E.g., anyone doing contract work can ask you for a large amount of money upfront, and afterward, ask for a lesser proportion after you've refused. This works since, according to me, the smaller appeal appears comparatively rational after the larger demand.

YOU INTERROGATE YOURSELF

Frequently, the term "gaslighting" is used to recognize manipulation that causes people to question themselves, their actuality, consciousness, or thoughts. A dishonest individual can distort what you're saying to make it about them, hijack the discussion or make you sound like you've done something bad when you're not entirely sure you've done it.

If you're being emotionally manipulated, you may experience a false sense of shame or defensiveness — like you utterly lost or had to do something wrong when, in fact, that's not the case.

"Blame the manipulators. They are not taking responsibility for this."

THE RELATIONSHIP MAKES YOU FEEL SCARED

Here's a general tip: if a relationship is built entirely out of a foundation of fear, then you know that it might not be a good one to be in. It's normal to feel intimidated or even somewhat fearful of certain people. Perhaps, you might be meeting someone you admire and idolize. To feel somewhat intimidated by that individual is okay to a certain degree. However, when you start building a close and intimate relationship with the person and the fear still doesn't go away, then that is a bad sign.

Manipulators understand fear very well, and they know how to use it against those who don't have good control over their phobias. For instance, say you've been planning something for a while and the person always comes up with last-minute changes that give them what they want, they are utilizing your fear of losing something. In this case, the time and emotional attachment were spent making and almost executing the plan. They will utilize the fear that you have of them into making you do things that would benefit them, even if it means compromising your well-being. This is why you should always be wary of relationship environments that reek of fear and intimidation.

YOU ARE MADE TO FEEL GUILTY ABOUT EVERYTHING YOU DO

Somehow, you are made to feel guilty about everything that you do. When you are in a manipulative relationship, nothing that you ever do will be right or correct.

Even when you have the best intentions and you are sure about your execution, there's still always something for you to feel bad about. Generally, a manipulative individual will avoid making you feel validated for your efforts or your actions. This is because they want you to feel like you need to work harder to be worthy of their attention and approval.

This is a tactic that is designed to bully a person into thinking that they're not doing enough so that they feel pressured to become better. It's a kind of negative reinforcement that is quite common in a lot of abusive relationships all over the world. It's the same way a boss would tell a worker that their work is mediocre to get that worker to keep on trying harder out of guilt or shame.

YOU OFTEN QUESTION YOUR OWN BELIEFS

Gaslighting is another common technique that is usually employed by manipulative individuals to distort an individual's view of reality. As a victim, you are made to doubt your own beliefs and perspectives on things so that you grow reliant and dependent on another person. Essentially, you are made to distrust your senses and instincts so that you will be forced to cling onto someone else to help you stay grounded and sane.

Manipulative individuals are so good at distorting the facts and stretching the truth to the point that they make lies seem believable even when they're completely outrageous.

In essence, they are just thrusting their version of "reality" down your throat.

You are made to feel like there are always strings attached

Nothing you ever do in this kind of relationship will come without any strings attached. You just get the sense that if you will be on the receiving end of some nice treatment, it's never something that you can just take at face value. You notice that there's a pattern that's emerging here whenever this person does anything that adds value to your life. You always just come to expect that there will be some kind of ulterior motives behind it. You would find it very difficult to just take a compliment or be on the receiving end of a kind gesture. You somehow get the sense that that isn't the whole story.

Your insecurities are always thrust into the limelight

One of the grandest ways in which a manipulative person would get you to become emotionally vulnerable would be to highlight your insecurities.

Naturally, as a human being, you have your fair share of insecurities.

We all do, and the manipulative individual knows this better than anyone.

However, instead of being sensitive and empathetic toward these insecurities that you might have, they use it as ammo. They will capitalize on these insecurities to make you feel terrible about yourself, setting the brain into more reactive, survival mode.

In psychology, whenever an individual engages in self-hatred or self-loathing, they find a strong power figure to whom they can cling onto. The manipulative master knows this, and that's how they will want to present themselves in your life. They will make it seem like you need them to be there for you because of how incompetent you end up perceiving yourself to be. When you're with a manipulative person, you will constantly be bombarded with reminders of your vulnerabilities. Sparking insecurities or questioning people's identity to create "issues" people didn't know they had and then allaying these insecurities by offering the solution, is also a commonly used tactic in marketing.

YOU'RE STILL EXPECTED TO FORGET

If you don't go along with what they want, then they'll make you feel guilty. Even if you did have every right to say no. If you feel pressured continuously or compelled to do something you don't want to do, you are being manipulated. If you're afraid to say no, then you're manipulated. If you feel bothered to go along with the demands of someone else, you will be manipulated. Manipulators are experts in playing the victim card, and they will play it to make you feel as guilty as possible, as if you're doing something wrong because you've chosen to tell them no.

DOUBTING YOUR OWN JUDGMENT

You still find yourself questioning your own judgment every time you are around a particular person. Suddenly, after having a conversation with a manipulator, something you were so sure of a minute ago, fills you with doubt and makes you second guess your own decisions. Present them with an idea or an opinion, and they will somehow find a way to twist and turn it around, making you uncertain and uncomfortable. Spend enough time with them, and they will make you feel unworthy as if you were a complete failure, and nothing you could ever do is the right choice.

You're just blaming yourself

Even though you've done nothing wrong, you're blaming yourself somehow. That one dishonest friend who always has an explanation for their bad conduct or poor judgment is not your friend, as they are always making you the scapegoat. This one friend is a manipulator. It's your fault; you made me believe I should, if you thought it was a bad idea, I wouldn't have done it. A dishonest "friend's" trademark is when you're in the mix somewhere, and they are the ones who made you feel like you're wrong.

Glaring and Unbelievable things

They do glaring and unbelievable things, and then they try to convince you that what you saw wasn't true. What you saw couldn't be what you possibly think. It is because it doesn't look like you will do anything like that, and he would have to be a real idiot to do something like that to you. He wants to minimize his action and play ignorant like he has no idea what it is, and that you are tripping, because both of you are just friends. He also tries to make rude remarks in the name of humor.

Why you are manipulated

An inability to set boundaries or to say "no."

Those who are easy to manipulate are generally so scared of confrontation that they are not willing to spark an argument by being resistant or by voicing their opinion. This specific trait is easy to exploit for obvious reasons—if they just cannot say no, you can burden them with favors and expectations, and anticipate no resistance in return.

Honesty and compassion

Being honest makes you particularly manipulatable because your greatest weaknesses and loftiest aspirations are all apparent to those around you. Compassion, on the other hand, is the driving force for the first point in this list. Being overly compassionate opens you up to manipulation by those who are willing to play the victim, as master manipulators always are.

FEAR

This emotion comes in numerous structures. We, as human beings, tend to fear losing a relationship; we may fear the disapprobation of other people; we dread to make somebody discontent with our actions. We additionally dread the dangers and outcomes of the manipulator's actions. Imagine a scenario in which they prevail at doing what they threaten.

GUILT

Today, we are clouded by the idea and responsibility that we should dependably prioritize the needs and wants of other people rather than our own. At times when people would talk about the right to fulfill their own needs and wants, manipulators frequently abuse us and endeavor to allow us to feel like we are accomplishing something immoral if we do not put their needs and wants in front of our own. Those individuals who are skilled at these manipulative tactics, would tend to define love as the act of fulfilling their needs and wants as part of your obligation. Hence, if we have an opinion that goes against their beliefs, we are manipulated into thinking that we are heartless; at this point, they will make us feel very regretful of our existence and would use guilt to manipulate us.

BEING TOO NICE

We appreciate being a provider, fulfilling individuals, and dealing with the needs of other people. We discover fulfillment. Moreover, our confidence would regularly originate from doing what we can for other people. In any case, at times when there is a lack of an unmistakable feeling of these and fair limitations, skilled manipulators can detect this in people who are easy targets of this phenomenon, and will use certain tactics to further their selfish gains.

UNCONDITIONAL LOVE

Those who are the absolute easiest to manipulate are those who unconditionally love the manipulator (parents, siblings, romantic partners, friends, etc.). The reason for this is that, regardless of the kind of treatment that they are forced to endure, they continue to love the manipulator. This love is an exploitable weakness.

BEING TRUSTING

People who are easy to manipulate believe anything you tell them, this is also known as "being too trusting." Some people are simply naïve, while others perhaps only see the best in the manipulator and refuse to acknowledge the uglier side—regardless of the reason, some people are easier to deceive than others.

BEING TOO POLITE OR RESPECTFUL

Manipulators actively seek out those who will not call them out in public, and who better to target than those who are too coy to say something when they are made to feel uncomfortable? Being overly polite also makes one more likely to agree to small favors which, as discussed earlier, makes one more likely to agree to larger and larger favors as time passes.

HOW TO AVOID BEING MANIPULATED

Similarly, it is just as important to know some tactics to avoid being manipulated yourself. The author of *Are You Too Nice? How to Gain Appreciation and Respect*, Ni Preston, developed eight techniques to avoid being manipulated.

The first technique he described is by far the easiest to abide by. It simply involves practicing the art of saying "no." If you feel uncomfortable with what is being asked of you, firmly say no. You do not necessarily need to be confrontational in doing this—a simple, "Sorry, I do not have time," will likely suffice.

The second technique is to set consequences. You need to handle a manipulator a little bit like you might handle a child: he or she needs to know the rules, and when he or she breaks these rules, there needs to be a "punishment." An example of how you could use this is by telling a person, "I am uncomfortable talking with you about that. If you continue to talk about it, I will report you to human resources." Manipulators do not want to get in trouble, so when trying to avoid being manipulated, make sure that you follow through on the rules and corresponding consequences that you have set.

The third technique is remembering that your time is your own, and you are allowed to take it. Manipulators will usually demand an answer to their requests immediately, in the hope of pressuring you into complying. You can circumnavigate this manipulative technique simply by saying, "I'll think about it." You don't have to follow a manipulator's timeline, and you are certainly not obligated to answer anything straight away.

The fourth technique involves asking manipulators probing questions when they make requests of you. Next time a manipulator asks you to do something for them, consider responding with, "Are you asking me, or telling me?" or "What do I get out of this?" or "Are you really expecting me to do that?" Chances are, you will catch the manipulator off-guard and perhaps even get them to withdraw the request completely (at the very least, it will force them to pause for a second and consider whether what they are doing is right).

The fifth technique is to avoid letting the manipulator make you feel guilty. You are not obligated to do anyone any favors, and thus, you have nothing to feel guilty about. Manipulators make their targets feel guilty in the hope that they will eventually feel so bad about themselves that they will give in to the manipulator's will.

The sixth technique is to keep your distance. If you know that somebody is manipulating you (or trying to), do not give them any opportunities to do so by spending time with them. It is honestly good advice just to give a manipulator a wide berth and to avoid getting pulled into their games altogether.

The seventh technique is to know your rights. Manipulators will go out of their way to violate them. Remind yourself regularly that you have the right to be treated with respect, to set your own priorities, to have a differing opinion, and to express your feelings.

The eighth, and final, the technique is to confront the manipulator. Publicly. A manipulator will generally avoid the public eye, and by calling them out, you are likely to put them off trying to manipulate you ever again.

DEALING WITH A TOXIC PERSON

Other indications to keep a watch out are if the individual is constantly condescending, compulsively in desire, or unwilling to take accountability or say sorry for one's behavior.

It may be anyone who regularly takes narcotics or alcohol, lies or wants you to lie about them, regulates or demeans what you've been doing. A toxic man's life is always personally, emotionally, financially, physically, or interpersonally out of balance.

Setting Boundaries to Eliminate Manipulators

"If you feel unnoticed or misunderstood and feel manipulated or compelled to do stuff that is not even 'you,' then you may be affected by a negative human." Toxic individuals can make you question yourself or unconsciously do something that you wouldn't normally do—you might feel a need to be fit in or cool or get approval. Every situation is different, but by influencing people to do something, toxic individuals may have a detrimental effect on others. They try to generate turmoil by negative behaviors: to use, to lie, to steal, to control, to criticize, to bully, to manipulate, to create conflict, and so on.

Effect of Toxic People on Your Life

Toxic individuals can impact all aspects of people's lives, and we are always oblivious to that. We feel sympathy for them. The myths they inflict on us are accepted and rationalized. And this, in exchange, changes how we look about our values and ourselves. Toxic individuals are happy to drive happiness down from the stuff we previously enjoyed, such as jobs, relationships, interests, and even our self-love.

Dealing with Manipulators Who Are a Permanent Part Of Your Life

If a manipulator had been in your life for a while, you might have already ceded some level of control over your life to him by now, so you have to start by regaining that control. First, you have to create and enforce boundaries in your life.

To set and enforce boundaries, you have to assess different areas of your life and set firm limits in all of those areas. You have to draw a line, and you have to make it clear to the manipulator that he or she is not allowed to cross that boundary. For example, you can set aside some "me time" and tell everyone that they are not allowed to bother you during that time.

Setting boundaries will help you reestablish the priorities in your life. If you have been a victim of manipulation, chances are the manipulator has spent months or even years establishing control over your life, so that by the point you know what's going on, he may have replaced your priorities with his own. You may find that you are using all your free time to do things he likes, and your interests have taken a back seat to his.

When you find yourself in such a situation, bouncing back can be hard, but it's going to require a lot of willpower and commitment on your part. Take control of your own life. Create a list of all your values and reexamine all of them. Look at your belief system, and question everything that you believe about yourself; did you always hold those beliefs, or did you acquire them over time as you got closer to the manipulative person?

If you notice that your time is spent doing things that don't interest you, your belief system has been infiltrated by ideas that aren't originally yours, and that your long term values no longer seem to be the driving force behind your life, you need to create new boundaries and rules for yourself to keep the manipulative person from controlling you.

You need to disconnect from manipulative people, especially the ones whose machinations have caused you (or could potentially cause you) serious psychological or physical harm. One mistake most victims make is that they assume that they can change the manipulator. They convince themselves that if they spend enough time with the manipulator, he will fall in love with them, and he will be open to treating them better. However, in the end, the opposite happens. Instead of the victim changing the manipulator as she may have hoped, it's the manipulator that changes her, and not for the better. She starts accepting the emotional abuse, and little by little, she makes concessions about her values and principles, until, in the end, she is a completely different person. She becomes more subservient, and she starts making excuses for the manipulator.

So, once you notice that someone is manipulating you, the best choice you have is to disconnect from them. If a clean break is possible, you should go for it. However, in situations where it's a lot more complicated (for example, where you have children together) a clean break might not be possible. Even then, spending some time away from the manipulator can help you re-enter yourself so that you can remember what your real values and priorities used to be.

Chapter 2

What Is Manipulation? Why Manipulation Is Wrong & Why People Manipulate

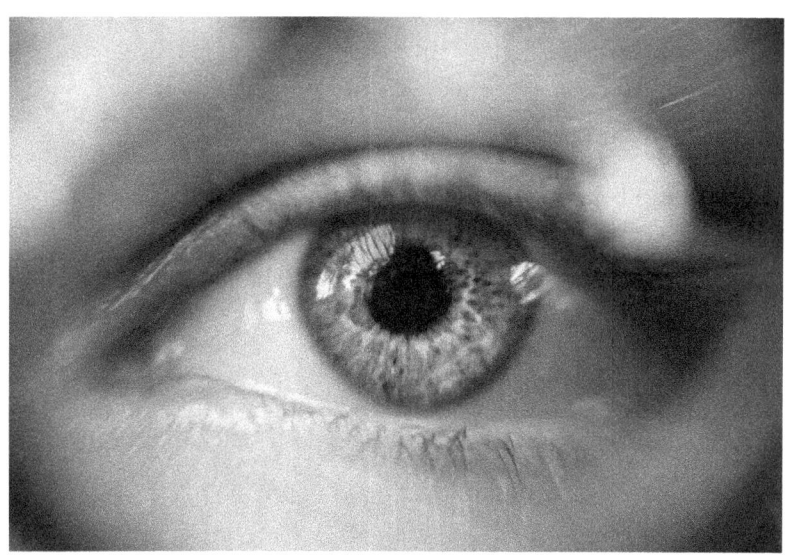

WHAT IS MANIPULATION

Manipulation is - in psychology - a method deliberately implemented to control or influence the thinking, choices, actions of an individual, via a relationship of power or influence. The methods used to distort or orient the perception of the interlocutor's reality by using, in particular, a relationship of seduction, suggestion, persuasion, involuntary or consented submission.

Manipulation is part of the daily lives of civilizations. In the modern West, power systems, conflicts of interest, power struggles are omnipresent: it develops from self-awareness, language, and the hierarchy of society which produce a large number of interactions from which everyone wants to benefit from. It is a learned skill that forms part of the culture, and which everyone knows and uses in their personal or professional life, in a positive or negative, conscious, or unconscious way. In such a civilization, any communication (body language or oral language) can, thus, be a form of influence or manipulation.

A manipulative person uses indirect means to make a person change their actions or thoughts. Some of the indirect tactics include persuasion and brainwashing. In persuasion, a person does not force you to do something, but they try to convince you to do it. A good example of persuasion in marketing. Although an advertisement is aimed directly at convincing you to purchase a certain item, you are not in any way forced to purchase it. The choice to buy it or not is in your hands. The only aspect that an advertiser works on is to ensure that you see the beauty of the item. The advertiser will only tell you about the good aspects of the item you are trying to buy without mentioning the negatives. Even those who choose to mention the negatives, also try to show them as slightly positive aspects. This is an indirect way of luring someone into making a purchase.

Manipulation is a way of socially influencing you into doing something you did not necessarily want to do. However, this does not mean that social influence in and on itself is something bad. Social influence can be used for a good cause. You can influence someone to stop taking drugs or change some unhealthy habits. When you persuade a person to do such actions, it cannot be termed as manipulation. Social influence only becomes a manipulative habit if it is aimed at benefiting the influencer. If you can persuade someone into taking another job just to benefit from their salary, you are a manipulator. Most manipulative individuals do not deem their actions harmful in any way. When a person is using manipulation tactics, they aim to benefit without directly being seen as a bad person. In most cases, a manipulative person will lure you into doing something bad and end up blaming you for it. In simple terms, a manipulative individual uses other people as puppets. You are just a tool that the manipulator uses to achieve a certain goal. A manipulative person can use you to steal money and end up putting all the blame on you.

There is a whole range of methods ranging from cunning, an action that can be legitimate, to the most degrading forms of psychic manipulation, including all kinds of lies. Manipulation as a scientific concept is mainly studied in social psychology and philosophy.

Mental manipulation induces a power relationship that results in the psychic control of a person. More precisely, it is "the modification of an individual's mental state by another to make him do something." This can be summed up in "fabricated consent."

In social psychology, the term "conditioning," is a word that appeared in the 14th century and developed following Pavlov's work. "Since then, and by extension, conditioning represents the mental or psychic conditions necessary for the performance of a behavior."

We distinguish the influence of manipulation, even if they use the same tools and psychological springs. If they are just as difficult to detect: the impact implies a transparent motivation while the manipulation includes deception without any benefit. In psychology, manipulation is defined as a secret action of a person or group of persons. The whole art of manipulation consists in depriving the manipulated of his freedom without realizing it, and that he is persuaded to be free.

The propaganda or publicity-seeking to mobilize the behavior of short-term masses, sometimes is achieved using irrational means. According to its use as a weapon of war, it is used as propaganda to manipulate public opinion. Disinformation is "probably one of the most difficult manipulations to detect and identify," and it is one of the main weak points of the information society.

The packaging is in the long-term by forming habits and playing on emotions. The indoctrination educates, also for a long time, addressing the beliefs and intelligence.

THE MANIPULATION ETHICS — COULD MANIPULATION BE GOOD AND BAD?

At the mention of the word 'manipulation,' negative connotations associated with this term is what immediately springs to mind. Manipulation means taking advantage of someone else by unscrupulous and underhanded tactics. Manipulation means theft and lying outright. Manipulation is unethical. Through the years, the word has had a poor reputation, and even the phrases used to characterize deception in play, depict an image that is quite nasty or negative. "She's got him wrapped around her little finger," "I told my boss exactly what he wanted to hear," "He's got a reputation for being a heartbreaker," "I spoke to my buddy about doing what I wanted." These traditional manipulative scenarios don't make a positive difference to the situation for the parties involved in the transaction. It makes the manipulator greedy, self-serving, deceitful, and unconcerned about manipulating someone else for their gain, and it makes the one being manipulated seem stupid, ignorant, and maybe even weak to "allow" himself to be so easily fooled.

Manipulation has always been seen as a cruel, smart, yet cunning act and always where one person ends up being manipulated. Manipulation is seen even more negatively when it is clear that the conniving person has a heartless presence, disregarding the other's feelings and placing their own selfish needs above all others. Even worse than the manipulator, he exploited the other by pretending to be his friend and then using trustfully shared information against them. There is one fact that remains in our personal or professional lives. No-one wants to learn that they were abused. Nobody. Such uncertainty associated with it is hard and it is almost painful to imagine that there is a possibility that it might be used to exploit a positive, or even that it could bring about change for the better. Manipulation isn't all evil; however, shocking it might sound. There is manipulation all around us, and often you don't have to look very far to find evidence of it. Take, for example, marketers and advertisers, with their constant messages telling us to buy this, buy that, stop doing this, and stop doing that. They all try to influence our decisions one way or the other. However, what kinds of manipulation are trying to make us change for the better?

Ads that advise us to stop smoking and eat better are trying to exploit our choices, but they're trying to do so, in this case, to promote positive change. Quitting smoking is in your own best interests and it feeds well. Would this not make it a constructive way of manipulation, if it is for your good? Governments around the world are exploiting their people. Religion does, likewise. Yet, sometimes we choose to ignore it because it comes, so to speak, from a more "authoritative" source. Businesses are actively exploiting their customers by producing goods to raise their sales figures and then telling consumers, "without them, they cannot survive."

Whether it's utilized for "good" or "bad," manipulation is still manipulation, at the end of the day. Does any of us have any right to dictate the decisions or actions of another, even if we believe this is to their advantage? What makes the thought of manipulation so upsetting is maybe the fact that we don't like someone else trying to decide what we can door forcing us to do anything we wouldn't be inclined to do ourselves otherwise. Working managers try to manipulate their staff all the time, even if the good leaders do it to try and keep their staff motivated or performing their best. Active managers have mastered the art of motivational reinforcement skillfully and have turned it into an important method used to influence the success of their workers, driving them to achieve their objectives. That distinctive detail is the defining difference between what is classified as manipulation and what is called persuasion. Persuasion is a form of manipulation, but what distinguishes it from the negative image of manipulation lies in three things:

Aim.

Honesty.

What gain or positive effect the person you're trying to convince would have.

WHY ARE WE VULNERABLE TO MANIPULATION?

It is not enough to know the definition of manipulation; it is still necessary to discover the reasons for our vulnerability to manipulation. Of course, they are multiple and different from one person to another. In general, a first large group of explanations stems from motivation and its two great strengths: the avoidance of suffering and the pursuit of pleasure.

So, a manipulative person can motivate you to do whatever they want because they strike a chord with you and cause discomfort or an emotion that you don't want to feel. No one likes to suffer and feel guilt, fear, insecurity, helplessness, doubt, etc. So, in this case, you are being manipulated because you want to avoid suffering.

When your self-image is somewhat flawed; in other words, when you are unsure of yourself, of what you are, of what you want, manipulation can more easily cause you to doubt or guilt. For example, someone is sulking because you said or did something. To avoid the guilt, you say that you didn't mean it rather than endure this sulking (which is a form of passive aggression). Example number 3 above is a good illustration of this.

Besides, manipulation tactics can also touch one of your fears, such as that of being judged. No one likes to be criticized for being selfish, incompetent, ungrateful, or inhuman. It can also be the fear of hurting, not being loved, losing an advantage, losing affection, respect, a material advantage, or even your job.

The manipulative person may control your behavior by giving you the hope of some sort of gain. It will make you hope for an emotional advantage, attention, recognition, status, even love, or a material advantage such as career advancement, reaching your goals more efficiently, obtaining results, and tangible rewards.

Here you are in the other great force of motivation: the search for pleasure.

Of course, both types of motivation can coexist in each of us, depending on the context. However, you probably have one strategy that takes precedent over the other, some sort of mental program that influences your actions, no matter what decisions you have to make. Some are more motivated by the stick or by avoidance; for others, it is the prospect of gain that motivates them to act. Recognizing this underlying tendency in you may help you understand how you come to be manipulated.

WHY DO PEOPLE USE MANIPULATION?

TO GAIN WEALTH

People use manipulation to fulfill their desires in life. If you want money, you may use any means possible to get a good job. This is a very big motivation for most people across cultures. All over the world, people use manipulation just to get wealth. Since money is a valuable asset in life, it can give you access to most of your desires and most people will do anything just to earn money. Such motivation will make most people use manipulation.

TO MAINTAIN THEIR INTEGRITY

Many people use manipulation just to keep their names clean. If a person has evil intentions but does not want the world to see them, they will use manipulation. Narcissists use manipulation and blackmail to hide their weaknesses. A narcissistic person may even ruin your name in public or lower your self-esteem just to avoid showing the world that they are weak. Most people who are striving to maintain social authenticity may go to extreme limits in their drive to maintain social standings.

TO GAIN INFLUENCE

The other reason why people use manipulation is to gain influence. Social influence gives people power. Most people enjoy it when they have power and control over others. We have talked about the example of political leaders and how they use manipulative tactics just to gain control over the masses. Politicians will do anything possible as long as they gain control. It is normal for people to employ such tactics in their search for power and influence. A person who wants power and influence will approach you with lies and trickery just to gain power over you.

TO DOMINATE RELATIONSHIPS

Most people feel safe when they are the dominating voice in a relationship. It is normal for human beings to want to have control over a relationship. This desire to control a relationship may make a person want to manipulate others. Manipulation will help those individuals control their relationship partner and, thus, gain control of any related assets. The main reason behind that desire to have control is the fear of the unknown. If a person that is afraid of uncertainty is in a relationship and does not have clear knowledge of the future, they may use underhand methods to control the relationship.

SELF-SATISFACTION

In some instances, people who use manipulation are just looking for a way to satisfy their ego. Many individuals suffer low self-esteem and only find satisfaction in controlling others. You may be in a manipulative relationship trying to figure out what you did that was wrong. In some cases, you may do everything right, but still become a victim of manipulation. People practice manipulation just to feel satisfied and happy. Such people have deeply rooted emotional and psychological issues that need to be addressed by an expert.

WHAT ARE PEOPLE'S REASONS FOR MANIPULATING OTHERS?

Misery likes company: They do it because they gain satisfaction on an emotional level, from seeing the frustrated or negative responses of others. Certain people are so unhappy with their lives and themselves that they try to bring others down by creating problems for them.

It makes them feel powerful: Someone who is insecure and feels powerless will often try to exert power in other areas to make up for it. Getting others to do what they want gives them temporary satisfaction.

A lack of importance: Another reason why people negatively manipulate others is that they don't think that they are important. They believe that if they simply request what they wish for, they won't get it because they don't matter enough. So instead, they try to make us feel ashamed or guilty as a consequence for not doing what they want, as a preemptive measure from disappointment.

They are "too good" for some things: Other negative manipulators simply think that they are too good for certain tasks. They might see other people as below them, and therefore, expect those people to do the tasks that they don't want to do. This could be due to laziness, or simply an inflated sense of self.

Not knowing how to get things done: Some negative manipulators don't think that they are capable of gaining what they want, and instead operate under the assumption that they must convince and pressure others to do their bidding for them.

Selfishly "helping" others: Other negative manipulators convince themselves that what they are doing will help people. This is a common idea embraced by people who think that they know better than others what is best for everyone. Due to their beliefs that they have a higher intelligence or ability, they feel satisfied doing this and convince themselves that the people being manipulated are better off for it. The majority of negative manipulators are not bad people; they are simply misguided, inconsiderate, insensitive, selfish, and often, weak and insecure. Some of them believe that the people they are manipulating are not as valuable as themselves and that their desires and needs are not as important. This mistaken belief is what allows them to continue to act the way they do without considering the feelings of other people.

DIFFERENT TYPES OF NEGATIVE MANIPULATION

Turning your emotions against you: Techniques for manipulation vary widely, but usually, negative manipulators will attempt to get the feelings of others to work against them. They will try to do that by doing or saying things that are intended to stir up fear, anger, shame, guilt, or any other uncomfortable feeling. For example, they might insinuate that if we don't follow through on their suggestions or orders, something horrible will result.

Threats of future unpleasantness: They might also try to describe to you all the different types of unpleasant situations that could arise if you don't do what they want. They might imply or even overtly insist that something is our fault, responsibility, or duty, using ethics and morality to pressure us to come around to their ideas or demands. Some people will even throw every trick at us, warning us of the consequences of disappointing or letting them down.

Common phrases used: They may imply to us that we will be so happy if we do what they want us to do, or that we will make them very happy, and that they will love us so much. They may also use phrases like "You need to…" or "You must…" or "You should…" as a way to subtly pressure you into following through on what they are asking of you. They will say those phrases and others which insinuate great consequences if you don't follow the obligation they are giving to you.

What does each of the above methods and techniques share with each other? The person doing the negative manipulation doesn't offer anything of value in return for fulfilling their wishes. Instead, the victim gets exploited by a created power imbalance.

EXAMPLES OF MANIPULATION

There are many real-life examples of manipulation happening right next to you in your daily life. If you are keen enough, you may be able to notice how certain people use manipulation and blackmail to have things their way in life. It is common to spot such cases in the workplace. In family situations, manipulation comes in place when there is something valuable at stake. For instance, if a wealthy person dies without leaving a clear will, there will be many people fighting to take control of the properties of the deceased.

A real-life example of manipulation would be the case of Jonestown (Guyana). The story of Jonestown is one of the most documented cases of manipulation and brainwashing. The mastermind behind the story being Jim Jones, who was a religious/cult leader.

Jim Jones rose to fame in Northwest Guyana during the early 70s. His rise to fame was associated with supernatural affairs. Like all manipulative individuals, Jones managed to gather a small group of brainwashed individuals around himself.

One of the key characteristics of manipulative individuals is isolation, as we have already said. However, manipulators who wish to gain public influence and control large crowds of people, do not just use isolation. Most public manipulators use the inner circle approach. An inner circle is made up of people who subscribe to the ideologies of the manipulator. The ideologies are often deemed as right, and they are not seen to have anything wrong. This is an approach that most cultic sects take. When a person is introduced in the inner circle, they make them feel special, but at the same time, they are required to fulfill certain conditions. In most cases, you will find that members of the inner circle are required to pledge allegiance to the leader of the sect.

Like all sects, Jim Jones started creating a small circle of people who would later work as recruiters. The entire village of Jonestown started subscribing to the ideologies and teachings of Jones. After some time, many people subscribed to his teachings. The social pressure associated with the people joining the sect attracted even more people. The more people gathered to the sect, the more manipulative the man became. In the mid-1970s, Jim Jones pronounced himself as being a god who had come to rescue the people from their predicaments. Given that the case happened at a time when people were suffering from poor economic status, the leader took advantage of the situation. The poor villagers were drawn to him hoping that he was going to make their lives better. They gave their attention to him and allowed him to take control of all their lives.

Just like all manipulative leaders, Jim Jones did not care about the welfare of the people. He did not provide whatever he promised. Instead, he used his popularity to amass wealth from the victims. He lured the victims into giving him sexual favors and managed to control the whole village.

The story of Jim Jones climaxed with the massacre of over 900 people who followed the sect leader. The town was named after this merciless sect leader who did not bother to think about the welfare of the people. As a manipulative person, he did not mind killing 900 people just to get whatever he wanted. Although the story of Jonestown is an extreme case that looks at a person who showed sociopathic tendencies, it reveals the true character of a manipulative person. Most manipulators do not care about how you feel or what you think. They aim to gain and move on with life.

Chapter 3

Manipulation Tactics

BEST MANIPULATION TECHNIQUES

DISTRACTION STRATEGY

This is one of the most common manipulation techniques used by governments, political parties, world leaders, politicians, and other public personalities to divert the public attention from the vital problems by introducing continuous distractions and trivial/unimportant information.

This way, the public attention remains fixated on insignificant issues, while the true political and social issues are hidden under the carpet. It gives the public the illusion of being busy with something, though that something is of little consequence in their life. They don't have the time to think about the negative impact of important issues in their lives and the inability of their leaders to resolve these issues.

CREATE PROBLEMS THAT DON'T EXIST AND OFFER SOLUTIONS

This is another classic social manipulation strategy that is widely used throughout the world. It consists of creating an imaginary or foreseen issue to stimulate a specific reaction among victims of manipulation or the public. Then, the manipulator carefully introduces a solution to become the ultimate messiah.

For example, allowing urban violence to build and thrive initially or supporting terrorist camps. This can be followed by making people aware of how their security is the government's prime concern and how leaders will go all out to intensify security measures to ensure public safety.

You introduce a problem and then offer a solution without letting the victims realize that you were directly responsible for creating the problems. This way, you become the solution provider, who can get people to act in a desired manner.

THE PAINFUL REALITY

Let us consider a scenario to understand this strategy clearly.

Your boss urges everyone at the workplace to put in additional hours of work or to work during weekends. He or she may lead you to believe that you all stand to lose your jobs and the market is tight, which means that you have to step up and go the extra mile to survive. They will inform you about how other companies who weren't able to bag big projects couldn't sustain operation costs and eventually closed down.

The managers will convince you how a few sacrifices from your side can go a long way in saving the company's fortunes. Do you see what they are doing there? They are projecting their decision as painful yet necessary. They'll tell how they don't want you to stay late at work, but there's no other option if you want to keep your job or for the company to stay afloat. A majority will resign to the idea of working late.

TO PROJECT VICTIMS AS IGNORANT OR STUPID

The easiest way to get people to do what you want them to do publicly, professionally, or socially is to make them feel how ignorant or stupid they are or how they don't understand something. For instance, if you are looking to introduce new technology that will save labor costs and increase profits, you may have a bunch of people rebelling against it for fear of losing their jobs.

By using the ignorant manipulation tactic, you inform people about how they cannot comprehend technology which is designed to make things easier. You are playing on their lack of awareness or uncertainty about a thing. You are telling them that they aren't in a position to give their view or opinion about it because they do not have the right knowledge or understanding of these systems.

Again, you are replacing revolt with guilt, by making the victims feel like they are responsible for their unfortunate situation or their lack of intelligence/capabilities. Thus, instead of rebelling, workers blame or devalue themselves, inhibiting further action.

DROWN THEM WITH FACTS, INFORMATION, AND STATISTICS

Emotional manipulation doesn't work on everyone, especially in social and professional settings. Here, people are more inclined to follow the logic and rational arguments. Drown these folks in information by quoting research, facts, figures, statistics, and more.

Have numbers ready on your fingertips for any objections and clarifications. Overwhelm people with statistics, logical arguments, and research. Be armed with the vital information to "intellectually bully" people. Present yourself as the ultimate authority or the source of knowledge in a particular field. Cleverly present research that supports your stand or point of view. Take advantage of established expertise to the fullest.

One of the best ways to manipulate people with logic is to present research, statistics, and figures in a compelling and imposing manner. Focus on areas where you believe they may not have sound knowledge and question them about it. This establishes their weakness in their own eyes. They will realize that they have little or no information about this area and that you are more experienced or knowledgeable than them.

This will automatically increase your chances of getting them to do what you want. This technique works well during business negotiations, sales, social debates, and other social or public settings.

You gain a smart subconscious edge over the other person, which makes them more defenseless and open to listening to you. It creates a sort of intellectual superiority, which makes them feel inadequate and compels them to comply with your demands.

THE VICTIM TALKS FIRST

When you are getting another party to agree to your negotiation terms or buy from you, allow them to talk first.

This allows you as a persuader, influencer, or manipulator to establish their baseline. What are their strengths and weaknesses? What are their thoughts, emotions, fears, and behavior patterns? Are they more hesitant or self-confident? Do they appear extroverted/open or introverted/closed? Are they approaching the deal or sales with an element of hesitation? Are they overwhelmed by your presence? What does their body language reveal about them?

Allowing them to communicate first, helps you set a baseline for both their strengths and weaknesses, which can be utilized to get them to act in the desired direction. You can also prepare a list of questions that you can ask them to establish a baseline. The idea is to get them thinking in the direction of acting in your favor. For instance, if you are planning to sell insurance, you ask them a list of questions that help you establish their fears and, therefore, allow you to play on these fears for getting them to sign up quickly.

TWEAK THE ENVIRONMENT TO GAIN ADVANTAGE

You can use the right environment at the right time to ask for someone to do something for you. Debunk the theory that there is a place and time for everything and make the environment work in your favor.

For instance, if you are partying with a boss or coworker on a Friday night, instead of waiting until Monday morning to ask them for a favor, use the relaxed setting of a pub or bar. They'll be less guarded, more chilled out and relaxed, and in a more positive mood. Your chances of getting them to agree to the favor may be higher in a more relaxed setting, where they don't expect you to ask for such a favor. Change the setting of where you'd normally ask something like this to increase your chances of getting people to agree.

CRITICISM

This is whereby the manipulator uses tactics such as belittling, dismissing, and ridiculing you. This keeps someone off-balance. Negative criticism is directed at a partner that makes them feel unworthy. The act of criticizing enables them to gain control over you. The manipulator creates a narrative that there is always something wrong with you and you are not good enough. This kind of narrative makes you doubt yourself, often of what you feel and know. It reaches a point where you do not trust yourself.

USING FLATTERY, KINDNESS, AND CHARM

The use of kindness, charm, and flattery is often more damaging than you realize. The generous deployment of these techniques is known as a passive-aggressive type of behavior. The manipulator uses tactics such as gifting someone items, massaging their egos with flattery, and lots of compliments. One is left to question the real reason behind the compliments, expensive gifts, and paying lots of attention to the victim. These are acts done with ulterior motives, especially when they realize you are about to catch up on the manipulative state.

Bribery is also another technique of manipulating someone. It yields results when implemented. Bribery is a better technique than blackmailing an individual. You can even entice a friend with a better offer. The reward doesn't have to be of monetary value. It can be something that you would have done anyway or had already done prior. Perhaps, in the process of asking for help in your studies from a colleague, you can decide to offer her a lunch treat after studying in exchange.

LYING

Lying is normally used by con artists. Manipulators lie about everything they see, hear, or know. They create lies that are so complex that they tend to wrap people up in ways that they cannot differentiate between reality and fake life. These lies can only be disputed by checking for inconsistency in the stories. When the deal is too good, think twice before accepting an offer. Abusers use this manipulation technique as they do not have fears about it. Lying can be caught if the victim decides to do a background check on the sources of information.

HAVING THE HOME COURT ADVANTAGE

The process of manipulating an individual all depends on the level of control one has over the other. A manipulator will insist on meeting and having your interactions in an area he is comfortable with. This technique is used to gain an edge of control over someone by taking them out of their element. The places where you normally spend time, are usually his spots and not yours. These places include his office, house, vehicle, and hanging out joints. Such areas make the manipulator exercise his dominance. People are easy to control when he is uneasy with the environment.

This technique can be done away with when the victim makes it clear that meeting places should be where they are both comfortable. Restaurants and events to attend should be chosen by both of you. This leads to a partnership, breeding a healthy relationship in the process.

CARESSING THE EGO

Caressing the ego is most common in personal relationships. The manipulator caresses the ego of the victim by feeding her lies. The ego grows with time and in the end, the manipulator has you on his leash. This technique can be avoided if the victim of the act possesses humility.

MAKING UNUSUAL REQUEST BEFORE YOUR REAL REQUEST

This kind of manipulation technique is a slight "mind game" oriented. The tactic involves asking an unusual request, mostly of a higher degree. This throws the person off balance, as he wasn't expecting such a request. The manipulator knew how that person was likely to respond if he would have asked for the usual request such as money, favor, shoes. The victim was more likely to respond "no" because people's minds have been conditioned to avoid these tasks.

For instance, a salesperson knows approaching someone on the street and asking him to buy the items being sold would likely lead to no sale. The salesman would first ask the potential client to do something such as help him with directions. This will build a "relationship" with the person and makes them less likely to turn you down in your presentation.

VOICE RAISING AND IRATE OUTBURSTS

Manipulators raise their voices during arguments to intimidate someone. They believe this process of raising the voice aggressively or loudly can enable them to achieve what they wanted. In a relationship, passion can come out in different forms such as tenderness, cute smiles you give one another, laughter, and the desire to share warmth in the arms of another. Passion, however, should not be mistaken by angry unpredictable outbursts during disagreements. In marriages or couples where they tend to disagree with one another, it is not uncommon. There are various ways of handling conflict, such as, having healthy communication with your partner and not screaming or having temper tantrums. The aggressive voice is sometimes accompanied by strong body language.

The manipulator can also start to pick quarrels about non-issues. When this starts to occur, it's a display telling you there are items that need to be ironed out. There are forces at play. In a relationship, someone who's picking random quarrels is either cheating on the partner or looking to end the relationship.

INSPIRING FEAR OVER A PARTNER THEN RELIEF

This technique of manipulation tends to have a high rate of success over its victims. It normally involves making someone fear that the worst will happen by creating stories or giving out the wrong information. If the story does not happen, that person is likely to be relieved, and then he would be happy enough to grant you whatever you want. It's all about playing mind games with the victim.

DOING A FAVOR

When offered something, the humans feel indebted and generally try, as quickly as possible, to render a service in return to feel relieved, and thus, to let go of this feeling of obligation which they feel. This is mainly why many brands give free samples out of their products!

Consciously or not, in the human mind, incurring a debt brings about the fact of having to repay it. It is a rule which is the cement of the social bond, even in primitive human societies. However, the violation of the law of reciprocity is wrongly perceived, which makes it successful. This is why doing a service builds a bond of trust with the person and makes them more easily manipulated afterward. Angry, for owing someone something.

Another aspect of the rule of reciprocity: there is another principle, that of reciprocal concession. When an individual formulates a request that we refuse at first and reformulates his request, he makes a concession, and we, therefore, tend to respond with a reciprocal admission. To manipulate someone, ask for something rather than giving something. For example, ask for a small favor rather than rendering one. Or, ask for something you don't really want and then rephrase your request by pretending to make a concession.

USE THE PERSON'S FIRST NAME

The human brain needs to be able to name actions, things, and people. A name on a face and presto, it's no longer unknown. It is no longer "the mass." A first name, just like a word, helps make things concrete.

Besides, the first name is often the first word known and remembered by a baby. Therefore, this creates a unique connection between the baby's first name and himself—a kind of anchor. Suddenly, people who use their first name to address someone (even if they hardly know him), immediately seem more sympathetic and familiar. These are the two criteria that promote manipulation.

Have you ever heard someone say your first name without speaking to you? Yet inevitably, you turned around or at least felt concerned at that point. It was stronger than you! This is proof that there is a strong emotional anchor between your first name and you. So, the next time a stranger asks for your first name and uses it to formulate his requests, you'll know he's trying to manipulate you!

FLATTERY

Contrary to popular belief, flattery is a manipulation technique that works. However, you need to think a minimum of what you say.

If you respect this condition, then even if the person knows that you are petting them, they will be sensitive. However, be careful, this technique does not work if the person you are trying to manipulate does not think you are sincere.

Flattery is a technique of manipulation that belongs to the family of displays of love. We create a pseudo-spirit of family and belonging through embracing emotional displays, affection, and flattery. It is very beneficial because the individual immediately feels taken in by a new family.

GIVE A REASON

Our brain is hardwired to accept more of a request when it comes with a reason. Even if it's a shitty reason, "Can I go ahead of you in the queue because I have to go make photocopies afterward?"

Know that to manipulate people; you can choose to give a justification. Even if your argument is flawed, the person will be tempted to say "yes" to you. More, in any case, than if you don't bother to argue.

STEP IN THE DOOR

The foot in the door is a well-known manipulation technique. Asking someone for a small favor is a great way to build a persuasive "dynamic." Then you present your "real" request to him.

This technique is a logical continuation of that which consisted in being rendered a small service. Except that here, instead of playing on reciprocity, we are playing on commitment and consistency.

If the person answered yes to your first request or did you a little favor, you could ask for something more substantial. The person is expected to say yes because they want to justify the fact that they have already helped you and because you have built a pseudo-relationship of trust.

THE DOOR IN THE NOSE

The trick relies on the power of human guilt. It is the reverse of the foot in the door. Here you will ask for something huge or ridiculous to get a no.

When the NO answer finally comes to you, you present a second request, which is more reasonable (but genuine from the start, of course).

By the way, if by some mystery the person accedes to your first "huge" request, so much the better! But more often than not, she will accept the second instead.

THE RED SCARF

The red scarf technique involves reluctantly pretending to refuse something to have a better chance of getting a reward (which you wanted from the start).

Example to better understand is a divorce where we would insist on having the dog. At the last moment, we would reluctantly pretend to give it up in compensation for something else like a trinket (which we wanted from the start). The other party will leave it to us, thinking they've won.

THE GUILT

Guilt is a technique that can be used to manipulate someone. But be aware that, depending on who you come across, it can also irritate them and have the opposite effect.

To make someone feel guilty is to say to them, "I thought I could count on you," and that sort of thing.

Chapter 4

How to Help Someone Being Controlled

You will encounter manipulative people in your life – there is no question about it. So, you must learn how to deal with them. There are two kinds of manipulators that you will deal with; those you can avoid (strangers, casual acquaintances, etc.) and those who are a permanent fixture in your life (family members, close friends, colleagues, etc.).

When it comes to strangers and casual accountancies, once you notice that they are manipulative, you can keep your interactions with them at a minimum. However, if it's someone close to you, dealing with them will be a lot more complicated, and it requires a lot of effort and commitment on your part.

When you encounter a manipulative person, the most important thing you can do is to keep your emotions in check and try to be as logical as possible. So, first, you need to stay calm. Manipulators know that they are more likely to get what they want when you react emotionally, so they'll do whatever they can to get a rise out of you or to emotionally destabilize you in one way or another.

So, the best thing you can do at that moment is to take a breath, calm yourself, and try to think clearly. For example, when a manipulator asks you to do something, he will keep pushing you because he wants you to say "Yes" right away. He wants you to make an instant emotional decision because he knows that if you take your time, think things over, weigh the pros and cons before making a decision; you are more likely to choose an option that isn't in your own best interest. From this point on, you should be wary of any person who tries to force you to decide the heat of the moment.

Often, manipulators will try to create a sense of urgency (a salesman may try to tell you that he is running out of stock, or your partner might give you an ultimatum). Approach every interaction with the understanding that decision making (no matter how small it may seem) is an executive function and not an emotional one, so anyone who wants you to make an emotional decision is technically a manipulator.

To help people avoid making emotional decisions in the heat of the moment, some psychologists recommend the use of grounding techniques to deal with strong emotions. For example, if you feel stressed or anxious, you can ground yourself by focusing all of your attention on what you are feeling in your body at the moment (if for instance, your heart is racing, focus your mind on your racing heart;

this will keep your mind from racing all over the place, and it will help calm you down).

Once you have your emotions in check, the next thing you need to do is learn to say a firm "no." Many of us find it difficult to turn people down outright. Even if we have every intention of saying "no," we tend to go out of our way to soften the blow for the other person, to the point that it sounds to them as though there is room for bargaining.

Manipulative people are well aware of this vulnerability, and they use it to push the envelope as far as it can go. If they detect any hint of hesitation on your part, they take it and run with it; they'll try to guilt-trip you, shame you, threaten you, and do anything else they can think of to turn your "no" into a "yes."

You can try to use diplomatic language wherever it's necessary, but when you say "no" don't leave your statement open to interpretation. For example, if you say, "I don't think I can do it" instead of "I can't do it," a manipulator will take it as a challenge to try and change your mind.

When interacting with manipulators, you also have to learn to assert yourself. Manipulators will use lots of techniques to keep you from voicing your opinion or asserting yourself because they know that if you don't clarify your position, they will be able to co-opt your view and make decisions for you. During the conversation, when you try to make a stand on an issue, the manipulator will attempt to keep you from doing so by talking over you or interrupting you. When this happens, most people will let it go, and the manipulator will get it his way.

When manipulators want you to agree with them inadvertently, they may use "we "sentences to get you to feel like they are on your side, or even to speak for you in front of others. They may also speak in incomplete sentences or ask you to confirm every assertion they make because they are trying to make you more agreeable. To counter ensure that you never let anyone speak for you. Where the manipulator is involved, always make sure that you use "I" statements (e.g., "I want" or "I disagree") to create a clear distinction between you and the manipulator.

Manipulators seek to control others to get them to do what they want. They aim to exploit people by paying with their thoughts and feelings. With this in mind, it's possible to indemnify manipulators by their words, body language, and behavior.

If you meet a person who encourages you to reveal a lot of personal details while at the same time, he is going out of his way to hide details about himself, chances are you are dealing with a manipulator.

You can also tell that you are dealing with a manipulator if the person's actions don't match his words. Manipulators want to win you over, so they'll tell you what they think you want to hear. They'll make lofty promises at first, but when it comes to following through with those promises, they'll leave you hanging. So, pay close attention to what people say and what they do, and try to see if there is a disconnection between those two things.

Manipulators will try to alter your reality and change your belief systems. So, you should watch out for people who tell you blatant lies, even if the facts are easily verifiable. For example, when you are starting to date someone, and you catch them in a lie, but they keep insisting that their version of events is the true one, you can be certain that this is just the beginning, and that over time, their lies will just get more blatant.

Manipulators undermine your grasp on reality by telling constant lies. When you hear small but incremental lies over and over, you will get to a point where you start doubting your reality. In some cases, it can turn out so badly, that you start feeling as though you are losing your mind. This is a manipulation technique that's known as "alighting," and it's more prevalent than you might think.

When you notice that someone is telling obvious lies early in a relationship, your best course of action is to terminate that relationship and to get away from that person as fast as you can.

You can also tell if you are dealing with a manipulator if he or she plays the blame game or tries to make you feel guilty about pretty much everything. Emotional manipulators understand that they can leverage guilt to make people do things for them as a way of atoning for their mistakes. While manipulators may be good at hiding their true nature during the early stages of a relationship, "guilt-tripping" and the "blame game" are two of the things that they find rather difficult to conceal. To manipulators, these techniques are useful from the outset of a relationship, so they may use them without even realizing it themselves.

If something goes wrong on your date, manipulators will try to turn it into your fault, as a matter of record. Even if you are dealing with something that is entirely out of anyone's control, they will make logical leaps to conclude that you are the one to blame. Similarly, if something goes right, they will try to take credit for it. For every small thing that they do, they'll make sure that they point it out, and that you acknowledge that they are the ones who are responsible for it.

For manipulators, the point here is to keep score. From the very beginning of the relationships, they will make sure that there is a running tally of all the good things and the bad things, and they'll make sure that they are ahead on the list of good things, and that you are ahead on the list of bad things. This way, they can always have something to hold over your head in case they want to manipulate you.

So, when you start going out with someone, pay attention to their attitude towards scorekeeping. A scorekeeper is almost always a manipulator.

Manipulators have a way of overwhelming you emotionally, even if you have only known them for a short time. If you meet someone, and you get the sense that they are just "too much too soon," chances are you are dealing with a manipulator.

Love smothering is a common manipulation technique, one that you can detect early in a relationship. Here, the manipulator will shower you with gifts and signs of affection to make you emotionally overwhelmed. When you receive an overwhelming amount of affection, you are more inclined to lead with your heart instead of stopping to think things through, so this increases the chances that you will fall for a manipulator.

Romantic gestures are great at the start of a relationship, but if you feel that they are excessive, you should consider the possibility that you are dealing with a manipulative person.

COMBATTING MANIPULATION

Fighting off manipulative tactics and advances is more than just being able to identify it. Sure, it helps to know that you are being manipulated whenever that truly is the case. That means that you aren't being naive about your situation. However, it's also just as important that you can know the common tactics in dealing with people who seek to manipulate you for their gain.

You've already been exposed to the many faces of manipulation and the kind of impact that it can have on not just one, but on a large group of people. Now, you have to learn how you would be able to spot manipulative behavior in your everyday life. In addition to that, you have to know how you will deal with it whenever you find yourself in those situations as well. It's not rare for people to find themselves in manipulative situations and not know what to do about it. This is not by accident. Manipulative people have a way of compromising their victims' inhibitions and better judgment. That's why a lot of victims of manipulation can often feel paralyzed by the situations that they find themselves in.

If you know that you are in danger of being manipulated, then you need to do something about it. The will to act is entirely up to you.

Chapter 5

Dealing With Controlling People

HOW TO DEAL WITH A MANIPULATIVE PERSON

Psychological manipulation is always going to be a very loaded and heavy-handed issue. It can often be referred to as lying, deceiving, skewing, distorting, gaslighting, intimidating, guilting, and other such things. Manipulators can also take the form of many different people throughout your life. Sometimes, the person who is manipulating you might be a parent, sibling, boss, classmate, coworker, or romantic partner, among others. That's why manipulation is such a complex topic to handle.

It can take the form of various tactics, and it can also be employed by various agents. This is why it can be increasingly difficult for someone to be able to identify and deal with a manipulative person.

As long as you keep your eyes peeled and you make an active effort in seeking these red flags out, it shouldn't be a problem. Now, it's a matter of dealing with these people and managing their advances.

First, evaluate whether the person is more of a systematic or unconscious manipulator. The more systematic, profound manipulators are almost certainly beyond reach. They can have grand visions and don't care who they have to get by to pursue their goals, they may simply enjoy controlling others. Perhaps they have had childhood traumas and issues that lead them to exploit others for fulfillment. These types of people are more aware of it and aggressively pursue their manipulative traits. Whatever the case may be, if possible, keep your distance from these types of people. Indeed, the easy solution would be to cut this person out of your life, right? It can be so easy to just burn bridges with someone if you know that they have manipulative tendencies and that they would be so willing to advance their interests at your expense. That kind of selfishness should warrant a cutting of ties. However, it's not always going to be that simple. There will be times when the person who is manipulating you is someone you have a deep bond and connection with. There is even a chance they are not consciously aware of their behavior themselves. For instance, if your parent, partner, or friend is manipulating you, it won't be so easy to just break that relationship off entirely. This is especially true if you love your parents and you know that they love you in return. In this case, it's not just a matter of eliminating a manipulative person from your life. Rather, it becomes an issue of managing this individual.

When dealing with a manipulative person, you must tread lightly. Keep in mind that there is also a paternal kind of manipulation.

They might not have bad intentions, and they might take offense to the fact that you are accusing them of being manipulative. That is why you have to be extra cautious and sensitive when you broach the issue with them.

FIRST, BE SAFE

If you know that you are in danger whenever you are with this manipulative individual in your life, always make sure that there is a third-party present. You can never really know what they might do to you if the two of you are alone. So, before you confront them about your manipulation, make sure that you have someone else in the room. You need that mediator; someone who would be able to help bridge the two of you. You can always call on a mutual friend, a shared loved one, or a trusted confidante. In more serious cases, you can even seek professional help from a licensed therapist. The point here is that the confrontation process should never be conducted recklessly. Your safety is always going to be the priority here and a lot of the time, that means having someone else in the room to be with you.

TAKE A DIPLOMATIC APPROACH TO INITIATING A DIALOGUE

You can either choose to work your influence on them to lessen the negative effects, or you could just confront them. The initial confrontation doesn't have to be so hot and impassioned. The best approach to confronting this individual would be to be as calm and collected as can be. You want to make sure that you are taking emotions out of the equation here. Keep in mind that a manipulative person is always going to capitalize on the emotionality of a person. If you take that ammo away from them, then it leaves them very little to work with. In addition to that, it's more likely that they won't react in such a hostile manner if you take a more civil approach to initiating this dialogue with them. Using people's own words against them makes it harder to resist whatever it is you are asking them to do, if one claims to be selfless, then they would not partake in certain actions to begin with.

DON'T FIGHT BACK

If they will be hostile with you about it, resist the urge to fight back. You have to learn to pick your fights. Responding to them in a hostile manner is only going to result in you playing into their games. You don't want that. You want to make sure that you stay calm throughout. When they get emotional, don't invalidate these feelings. Their emotions might be very authentic regardless of whether they are based on distorted truths or not. A person can still feel angry about something that is a complete lie or fantasy. Keep that in mind.

SET CLEAR LIMITS AND BOUNDARIES

Once you have heard their side of the tale, it's now time for you to air out your grievances.

Again, you need to make sure that you keep emotions out of it. You don't want them to be invalidating what you're saying just because you're being hysterical. You want to be honest about it and be straightforward. You shouldn't be beating around the bush anymore.

Make sure that all of the skeletons come out of the closet. Be courteous, but also, don't pull any punches. No matter how uncomfortable it might be to speak honestly about your feelings, you will have to do so.

KNOW WHEN IT'S TIME TO WALK AWAY

Sometimes, you just need to be able to know when it's time to walk away. No matter how painful it is to cut yourself loose from someone who you love dearly, you still have to do so for the sake of your well-being. You should not be making any room for toxicity or manipulative behavior that causes a burden in your life, regardless of who it might be coming from. At the end of the day, the only real person who has your back is yourself. That is why you have to make it a point to protect yourself at all costs. If there is no way for you to find a peaceful means of coexisting with one another that doesn't involve any form of harmful manipulation that is taking value out of your life, then you need to be able to walk away from that.

Seek Apology for Your Part and Move On

You probably won't get an apology, but you also don't have to dwell on it. Own up to what you think you were doing, and then say nothing of the other allegations.

You Don't have to Beat Them

There should be no two people playing this game. Instead, learn to recognize the techniques so that you can practice your responses properly.

Know Your Basic Human Rights

In interacting with a psychologically manipulative individual, the most critical rule is to know your rights and understand when they are violated. You have the right to defend yourself until you harm others. On the other hand, you can forfeit those rights if you hurt others.

These are some of our basic human rights:

- You are entitled to be treated with dignity.

- You have the right to have your thoughts, views, and desires shared.

- You are entitled to set your own goals.

- You are entitled to say "no" without feeling guilty. You are entitled to get what you pay for.

- You have the freedom to have differing opinions than others.

- You have the right to care for yourself and to protect yourself against being physically, mentally, or emotionally threatened.

- You are entitled to build your own healthy and happy life.

Those basic human rights are your boundaries.

The culture is, of course, full of people who do not respect those rights. Psychological manipulators want to strip you of your freedoms, so they can take advantage of you and manipulate you. But you have the moral authority and power to announce it is you who is in charge of your life, not the manipulator.

AVOID SELF-BLAME AND PERSONALIZATION

Since the purpose of the manipulator is to try and manipulate your vulnerabilities, it is recognizable that you may feel bad, or even blame yourself for failing to satisfy the manipulator. It is important to remember that you are not the problem in these situations; you have been manipulated to feel bad about yourself so that you are more likely to surrender your power and rights.

BY PROBING QUESTIONS, YOU PUT FOCUS ON THEM

Psychological manipulators will inevitably make demands (or requests) of you. Often these "offers" make you be out of your route to satisfy their needs. When you hear an unreasonable request, it is sometimes useful to put the focus back on the manipulator by asking a few inquiring questions, to see if she or he has enough self-awareness to recognize their scheme's inequity. For instance: "Does that seem fair to you? "Sound fair what you want from me?" "Have I got a say in this?" "Are you asking me, or are you telling me?"

"So, what am I going to get out of it?" "Do you expect me to [re-establish the unjust request]?" You're putting up a mirror when you ask such questions so that the manipulator can see the true nature of his or her plan. If the manipulator has some sense of self-awareness, he or she will likely withdraw the demand and return. On the other side, genuinely pathological manipulators (such as a narcissist) will ignore your questions and convince you to get their way.

A "No" is a Complete Sentence

Practicing the art of communication is to be able to say "no" diplomatically but firmly. Articulated efficiently, it lets you stand your ground while keeping a relationship. Remember that your basic human rights include the right to emphasize yourself, the right to say "no" without feeling shame, and the right to choose your own happy and healthy life.

Take Time for Your Advantage

In addition to unreasonable demands, the manipulator will also often expect an immediate response from you to enhance their power and influence over you in the situation. During these times, instead of instantly reacting to the manipulator's appeal, consider taking time to your benefit and distancing yourself from its immediate impact. You can exercise control over the situation simply by saying: "I'll think about it." Remember how powerful those few words are from a buyer to a salesperson, or from a romantic prospect to an enthusiastic pursuer, or from you to a manipulator. Take the time you need to weigh the pros and cons of a situation and decide whether you want to discuss a fairer deal, or whether you're better off by saying "no," which brings us to our next point.

Confront Bullies

The critical point to remember about bullies is that they choose those they view as weaker, so as long as you stay calm and obedient, you become a target for them. However, inside a lot of bullies are also cowards. Once their victims start showing backbone and sticking up for their rights, the bully always backs down. This is true in schoolyards, in households, and offices as well.

YOU CAN SET BOUNDARIES

- When a manipulative person becomes aware that they are losing control, their tactics can become more desperate. It is time to make some tough choices.

- If you don't need to be close to that person, consider cutting them off entirely from your life.

- If you're living with them or working closely together, you'll need to learn strategies to handle them.

- Speaking to a therapist or counselor about how to handle the situation might be helpful.

- You may also be able to recruit a trusted friend or family member to help you identify the activity and impose limits.

SET CONSEQUENCES

If a psychological manipulator persists on breaching the limits and won't take "no" for a response, the outcome will be deployed. One of the essential skills you can use to "stand up" to a stubborn person is the ability to identify and demonstrate consequence(s). Expertly formulated, the outcome gives the deceptive person a pause and compels him or her to move from abuse to respect.

Conclusion

There has been lots of discussion about dark psychology, how and in which situations it is practiced most commonly and what the factors hidden behind it are. This is also considered to be a dark side of human nature, which is seldom exposed. Every human being, no matter how nice and positive they are, are always going to be evil in someone else's eyes. For the person whom you made suffer, you are evil, even if you deny it. Every person must evaluate him or herself and see if any of the hazardous or negative elements are found in them. You have to keep fighting your dark side so that it does not take control over you completely. Once you know to keep off that side, you will be able to identify it in others as well and can prevent yourself from falling prey to it. One must be aware of its indications and related signs so that people who have the qualities of dark psychology can be avoided. If you have fallen prey to dark psychology, then there is a chance for you to regain normality by assessing and evaluating yourself or by seeking medical advice.

Remember that deception is not always practiced on other people. We can often self-deceive to preserve our self-esteem. Telling ourselves that we can achieve certain goals when all the evidence points to the fact that we can't, is a healthy form of deception, but self-deception can lead to serious delusions.

Whatever happens in the novice stages of your path to becoming a master of manipulation and persuasion, you must remember your end goal. Ask yourself in the beginning why you want to do this and keep coming back to that when it gets hard. Never give up; you are to master these skills.

I hope that through this book, you have realized that brainwashing, manipulation, and persuasion depends greatly on an authoritative command of words. You might be able to list twenty manipulation techniques from memory; you may be able to get someone with little psychic resistance to go with your ideas.

You may have gotten to the end of the book — and you may have all the knowledge necessary to manipulate people — but you are just beginning when it comes to putting this all into practice.

Also, remember manipulation is classified into positive and negative (Egocentric and Malicious). The study shows how toavoid negative manipulators and try as hard as possible to stay in your lane. Work on the positive aspect of manipulation to help yourself and help others — best of luck!

www.ingramcontent.com/pod-product-compliance
Lightning Source LLC
Chambersburg PA
CBHW071544080526
44588CB00011B/1782